D0852299

flowers
PORTRAITS OF INTIMACY

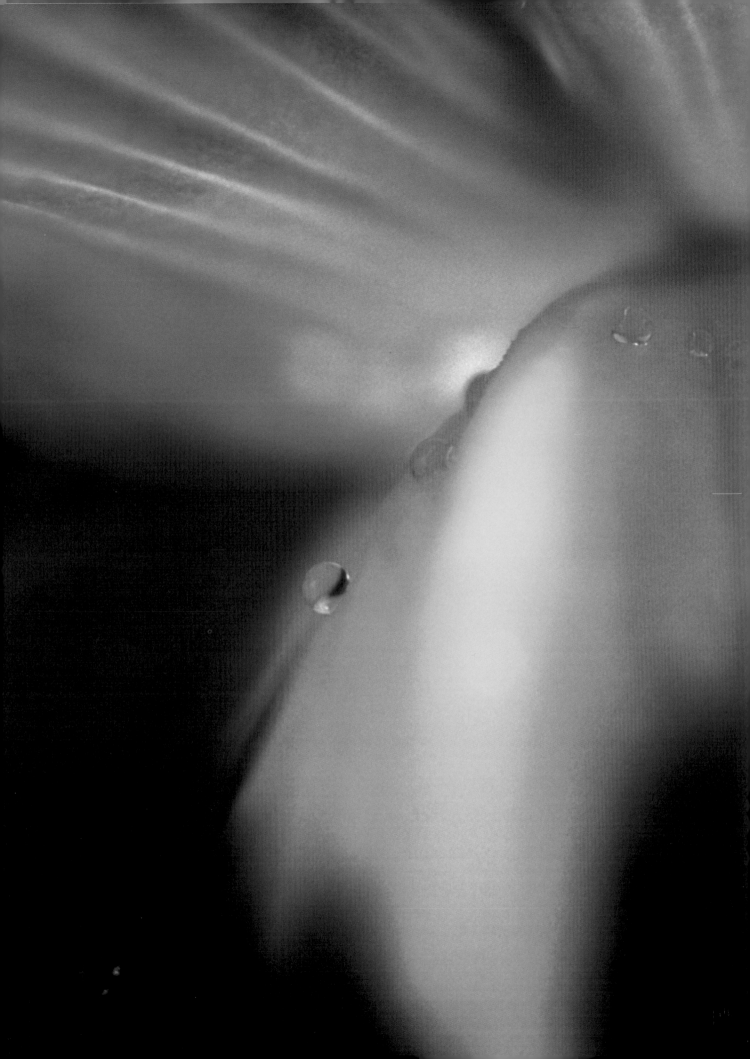

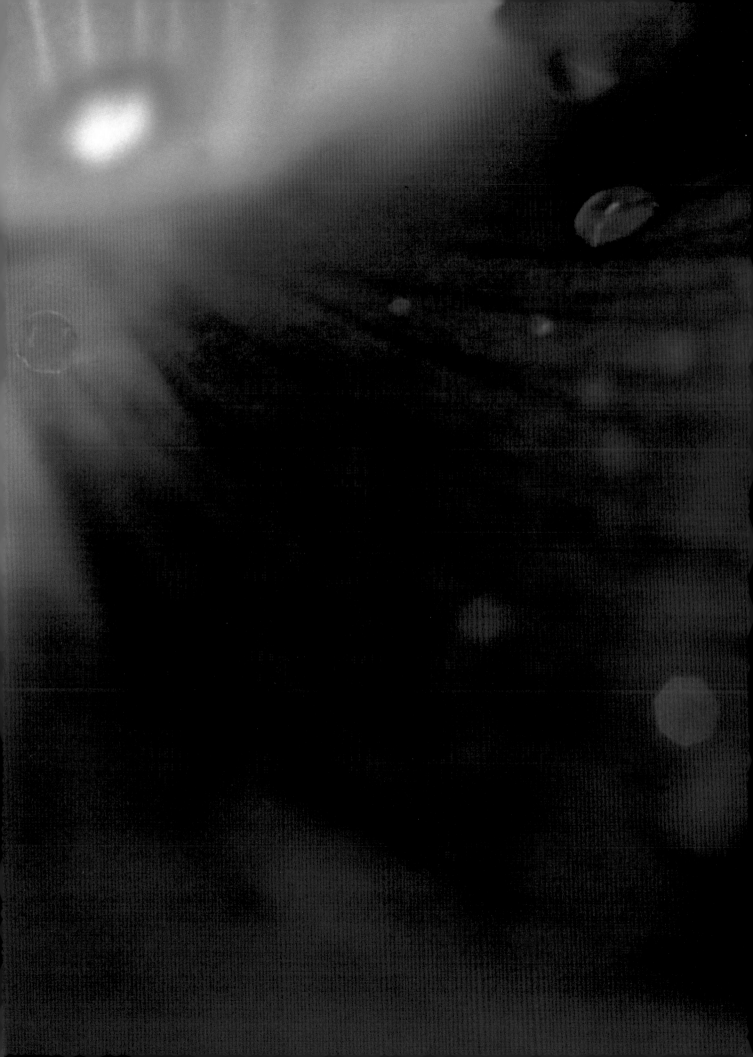

flowers
PORTRAITS OF INTIMACY

PHOTOGRAPHS BY
Adam Kufeld

INTRODUCTION BY REBECCA COLE

stewart tabori & chang
new york

Photographs copyright © 2001 Adam Kufeld
Introduction copyright © 2001 Rebecca Cole

All rights reserved. No portion of this book may be reproduced,
stored in a retrieval system, or transmitted in any form or by any means,
mechanical, electronic, photocopying, recording, or otherwise, without
written permission from the publisher.

Published in 2001 by
Stewart, Tabori & Chang
A Company of La Martinière Groupe
115 West 18th Street
New York, NY 10011

Library of Congress Cataloging-in-Publication Data

Kufeld, Adam
    Flowers : Portraits of Intimacy / photographs by Adam Kufeld ;
    introduction by Rebecca Cole
        p. cm.
    ISBN 1-58479-079-2
    1. Photography of plants. 2. Flowers–Pictorial works. I. Title

TR724 .K84 2001
779'.34'092–dc21   2001034190

Design by Paul Wagner
Text set in Perpetua and Today SB

Printed in Italy

10 9 8 7 6 5 4 3 2 1
First Printing

Pages 2-3: *Evening Primrose*
Pages 4-5: *Iris*
Page 6: *Dahlia*

For information and prints contact adamkufeld.com

Acknowledgments

Every book, it seems, is the product of the efforts of many. This one is no exception. First, I would like to thank my agent, Caroline Herter, whose initial enthusiasm for the photographs led to this book. I doubt it would have happened without her.

Many thanks to Leslie Stoker, my editor and the publisher of Stewart, Tabori & Chang, for her belief in the project and constant encouragement, and to Galen Smith, art director of STC, for putting it all together.

Thanks to Annie and Alejandro of Annie's Annuals in Richmond, the staff and owner of Magic Gardens Nursery in Berkeley, and Tom Perlite, owner of Golden Gate Orchids in South San Francisco, all in California, for generously allowing me to photograph their plants at will.

My gratitude also to Jane Norling, Myong Stebbins, and Claudia Bernardi for their opinions and artistic input.

To my partner, Darin Tennesen, for her consistent encouragement, insight, and support. Maybe I could have done it without her, but it certainly would not have been as enjoyable.

Zinnia

Introduction

*"Details are confusing. It is only by selection, by elimination,
by emphasis, that we get at the real meaning of things."*

—Georgia O'Keeffe

THE FIRST TIME I SAW ADAM KUFELD'S MAGNIFICENT FLOWER PHOTOGRAPHS I was with my best
friend's fourteen-year-old daughter and, I swear, we were both blushing. Not since my first
encounter with Georgia O'Keeffe's "Lily and Black" had I seen such primal erotic beauty in a
flower. I have been living and working with flowers for a lifetime, but I had never truly "looked"
at these seductive, powerful creatures until Adam revealed their most intimate crevices through
his macro lens and bold eye. His lens transforms all who look. Cast in the role of the pollinator,
we were seduced by the flower's beauty, intoxicated by the depth of color, and tingled by the
tactile wetness of the flower's inner self. No wonder we blushed. Is it not the natural response
to being seduced?

Adam has made a career of revealing worlds seldom seen. From documenting civil war in
El Salvador to recording everyday life in Cuba to showing the aftereffects of war on the people
of Vietnam and the children of Iraq, he uncovers the beauty and humanity of life rarely viewed
in clear focus. It is his passion for finding a new way of looking at things that makes all his work
as provocative as it is beautiful.

Born in New York's Greenwich Village to a mother with a Bohemian soul, long, flaming red
hair, and a passion for all things green and a father who was a member of the famous artists'
pack known as the "Group of Ten," Adam knew from a young age that he would never go to
law school. Surely it was his mother's weekly ritual of bathing the houseplants in the shower
and his father's early gift of a camera that sowed the seeds for this magnificent collection
of photographs.

From a botanist's point of view, the flower's sole purpose is to attract to itself the necessary
ingredients for reproduction. The flower's exquisite beauty, bold colors, decorative plumage,
intoxicating scent, and dripping stickiness of its pistil and stamens exist exclusively to attract
birds, bees, and other bugs to help pollinate. Only with the aid of a magnifying glass or a macro
photo lens can we experience this miracle of life. For a moment we become the birds and the
bees: we, too, are seduced. After all, we have borrowed the enticing power of the flower for
our own seductions. Long before diamond rings or candlelight dinners, humans used the scent
and beauty of flowers to woo true loves to courtship, marriage, and ultimately reproduction.
Perhaps the intelligence of flowers has been as underestimated as that of beautiful women!

Poppies, roses, zinnias, daisies, and anemones have given me a living, but I never really looked
closely at what gave them life. By focusing on their purpose—to captivate, to create—Adam
elevates the flower from decoration to a lesson of life: look deeper.

—Rebecca Cole

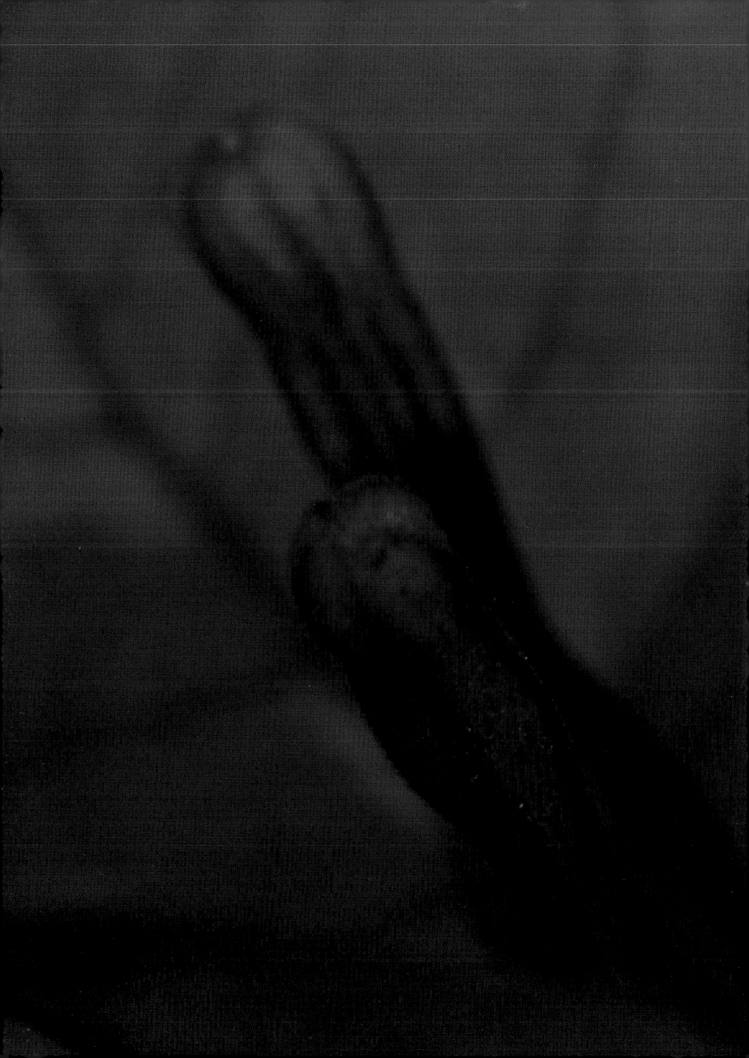

PRECEDING   ABOVE

Bougainvillea   *Dahlia*

Clematis

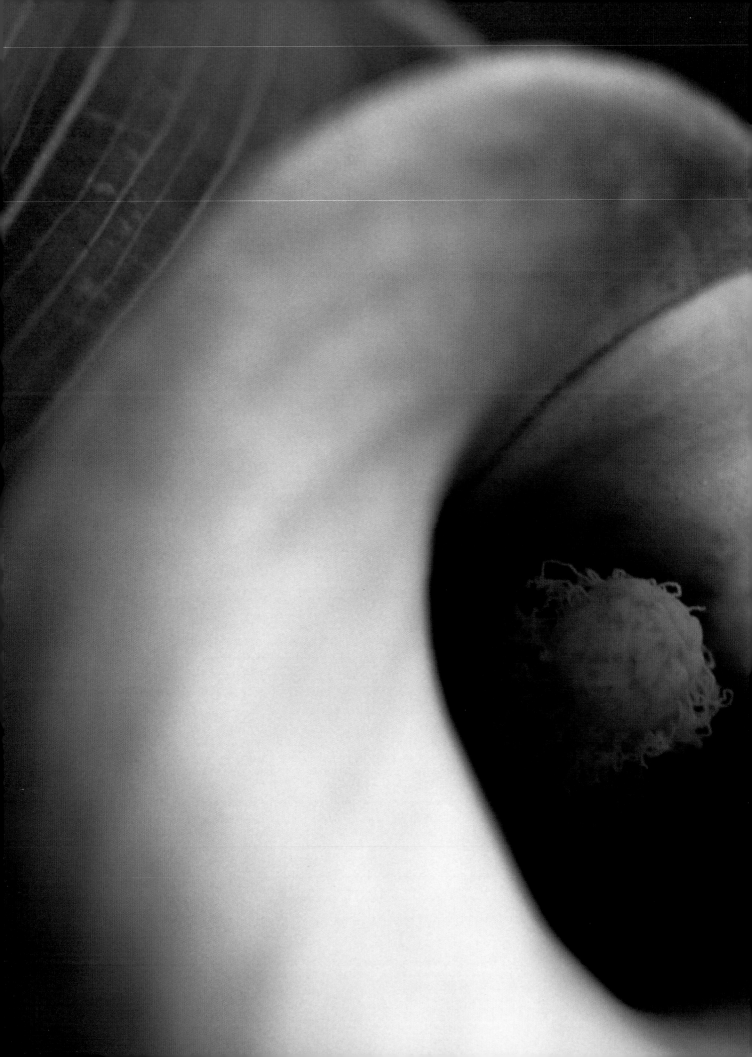

PRECEDING

Calla

RIGHT

Chrysanthemum

PRECEDING ABOVE

Lily *Rose*

Sunflower

Princess Flower

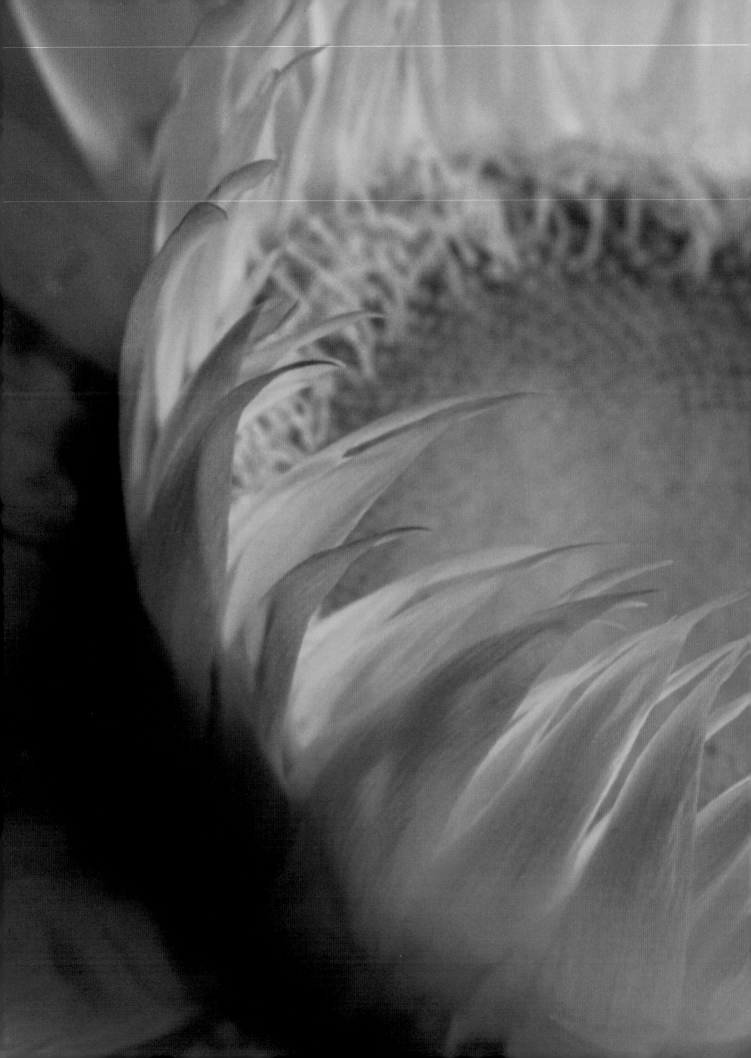

PRECEDING

Straw Flower

RIGHT

Rose

PRECEDING   ABOVE

Felicia   *Godetia*

ABOVE
Poppy

FOLLOWING
Dahlia

Cattleya Orchid

Delphinium

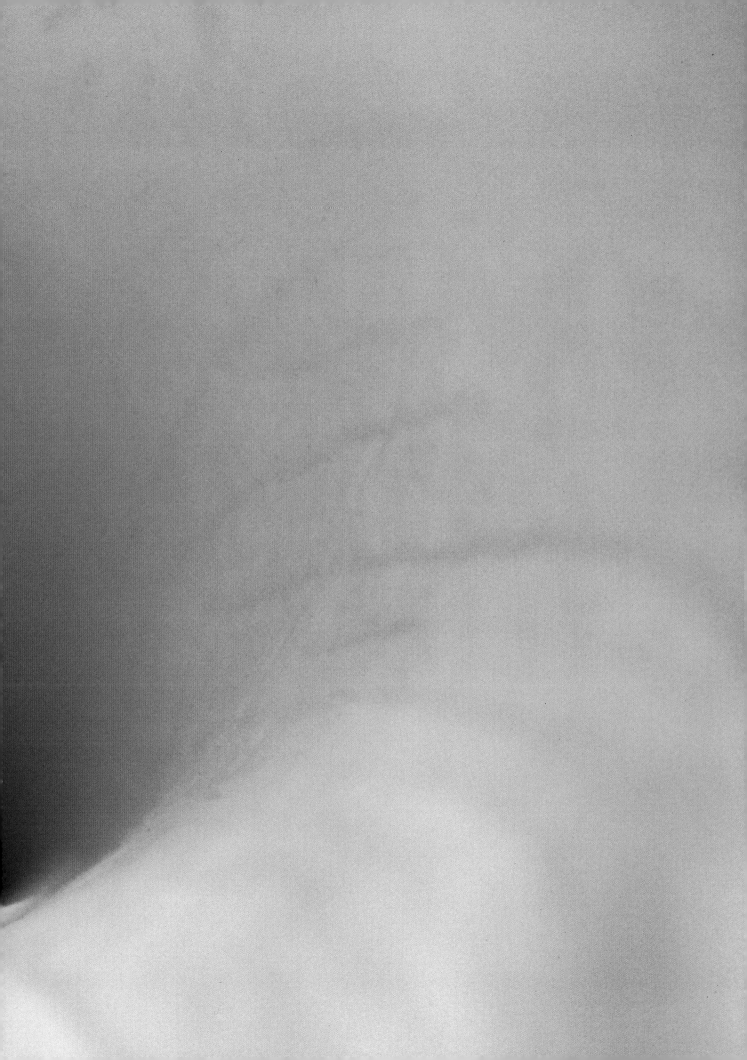

PRECEDING

Calla

RIGHT

Narcissus

Aster

Gloxinia

Paphiopedilum Orchid

ABOVE

FOLLOWING

Anenome   *Dahlia*

Gladiolus

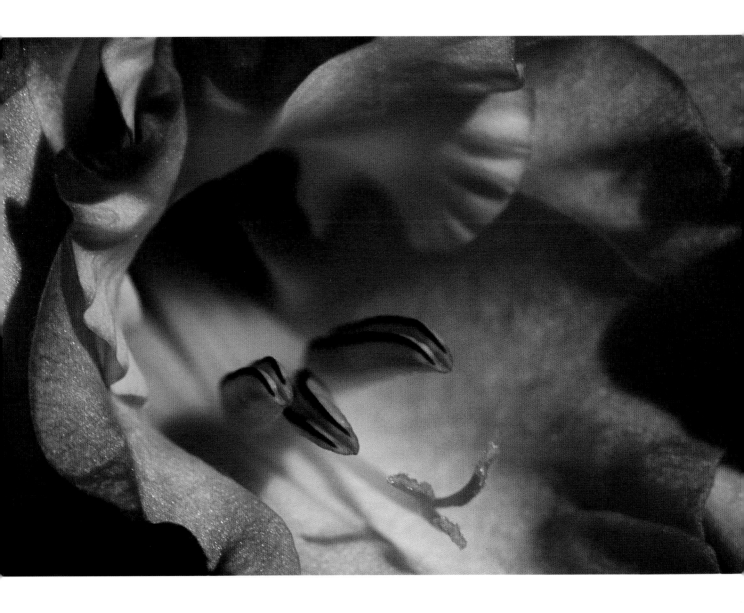

PRECEDING   ABOVE

Pimpernel   *Gladiolus*

Poppy

PRECEDING

Rose

RIGHT

Cathedral Bells

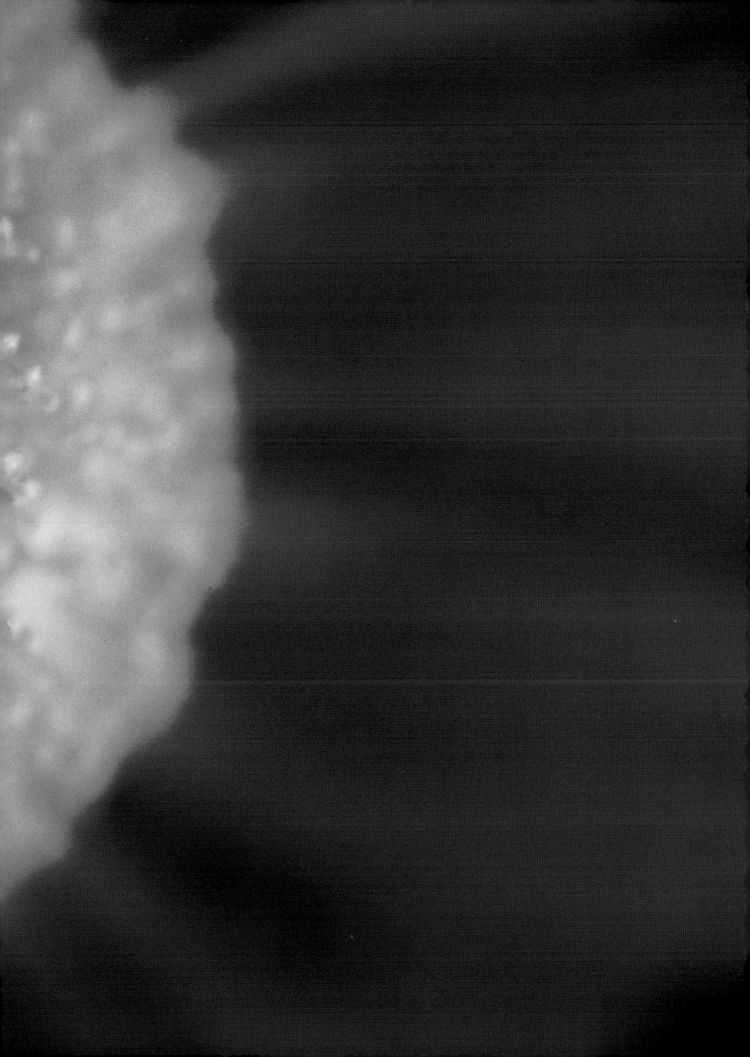

PRECEDING   ABOVE
Chrysanthemum   *Euphorbia*

ABOVE
African Violet

FOLLOWING
Odontoglossum Orchid

Lily

PRECEDING

Dendrobium Orchid

ABOVE

Hydrangea

Lisianthus

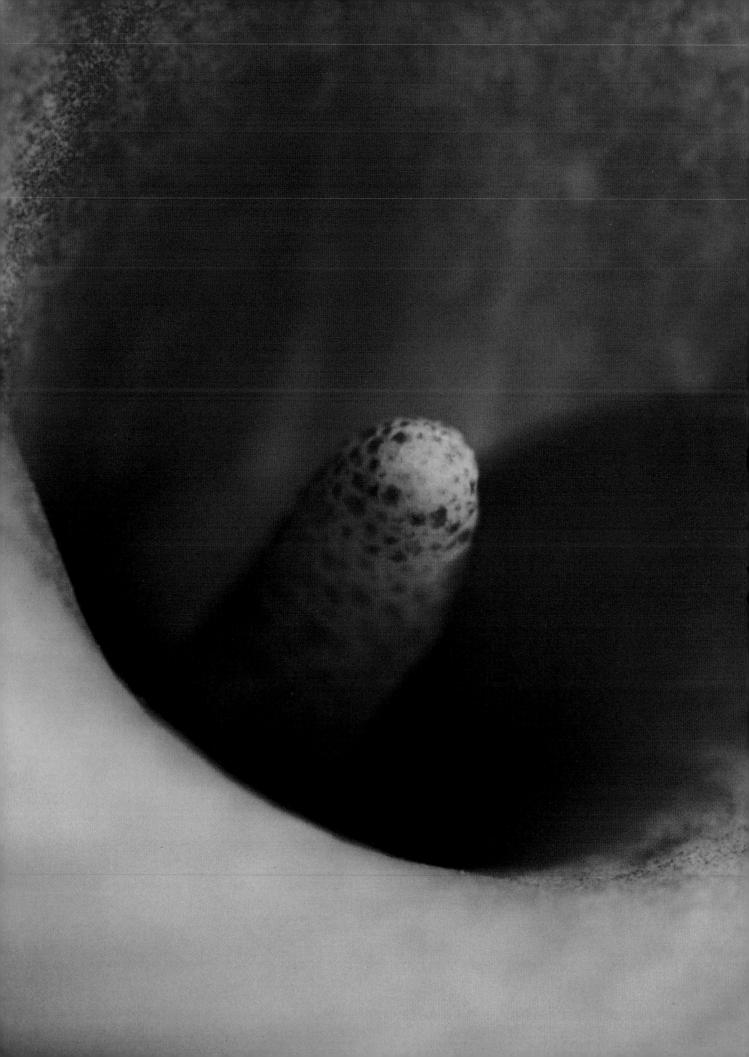

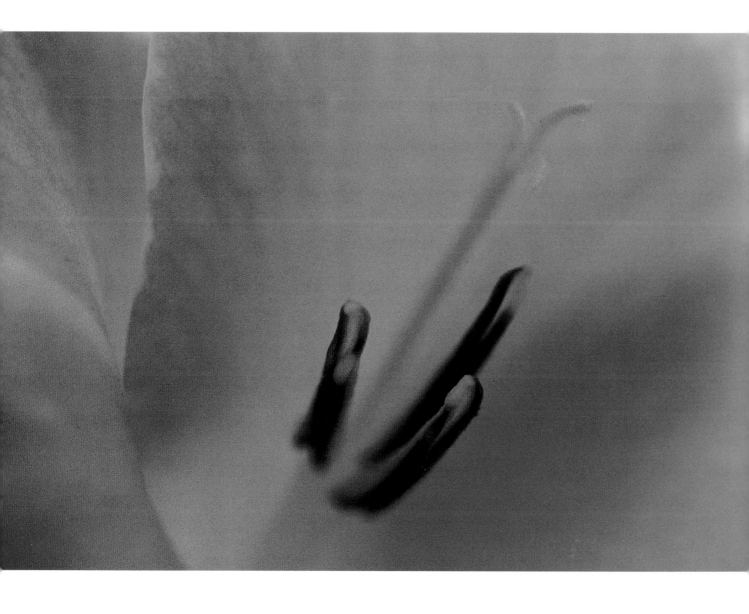

ABOVE

Poppy

FOLLOWING

Passion Flower

Pansy

PRECEDING   ABOVE

Rose   *Poppy*

Dahlia

PRECEDING

Lily

RIGHT

Cattleya Orchid

Cupid's Dart

Portulaca

LEFT
Daisy

FOLLOWING
Bird-of-Paradise